PERSONALIZED PROMISES FOR FATHERS

DISTINCTIVE SCRIPTURES PERSONALIZED AND WRITTEN AS A DECLARATION OF FAITH FOR YOUR LIFE

by

James R. Riddle

D1522103

Harrison House
Tulsa, OK

Verses marked KJV are taken from the *King James Version* of the Bible.

Verses marked NKJV are taken from the *New King James Version.* Copyright © 1982 by Thomas Nelson, Inc. Used by permission. All rights reserved.

Verses marked AMP are taken from the *Amplified® Bible.* Copyright © 1954, 1958, 1962, 1964, 1965, 1987 by The Lockman Foundation. Used by permission. (www.Lockman.org)

Verses marked NIV are taken from the *Holy Bible: New International Version®.* NIV®. Copyright © 1973, 1978, Zondervan Publishing House. All rights reserved.

Scripture quotations marked MESSAGE are from *The Message,* copyright © by Eugene H. Peterson, 1993, 1994, 1995. Used by permission of NavPress Publishing Group.

CONTENTS

INTRODUCTION

One of the wonders of God's Word is how much depth can be found in a single Scripture. One verse can speak volumes of information to us. Consider Hebrews 4:16. This verse alone contains promises of grace, mercy, forgiveness, boldness, closeness with God, answered prayer, spiritual power, and more. I've probably read it a thousand times, and yet each time I read it I am overwhelmed by the fullness of it.

It is my sincere prayer that your life will be changed as you declare each of these promises. Please, son of God, don't be duped into thinking that your hardships are God's will. He wants you to live a life full of joy, freedom, and peace. Read His promises. *They* are His will for you. Second Corinthians 1:20 decrees that every one of them is yours. Claim them today and enter into the abundant life that Jesus paid for you to enjoy!

THE BLESSING
OF ABRAHAM

The Book of Galatians declares that because of what Jesus did, the blessing of Abraham is now yours. (Gal. 3:13,14.) So many of us wonder just how God wants to bless us. I believe this is one of the reasons He gave us the example of Abraham. God says that we should be blessed in every way that Abraham was blessed, and more.

There is so much depth to the blessing of Abraham, but at the heart of it is a simple phrase, "I will bless you and you will be a blessing." I was studying this recently and realized that this is another way for God to say, "I want you to be just like Me." God wants us to have abundance so that we can use what we have to bless the world around us.

Take these promises into your heart and walk in all the fullness of them. Be a blessing to your wife, your children, your friends, and even the strangers around you. Show the world what it is like to be a son of the living God!

GENESIS 12:1-3 KJV

Now the Lord had said unto Abram, Get thee out of thy country, and from thy kindred, and from thy father's house, unto a land that I will shew thee: And I will make of thee a great nation, and I will bless thee, and make thy name great; and thou shalt be a blessing: And I will bless them that bless thee, and curse him that curseth thee: and in thee shall all families of the earth be blessed.

——— *DECLARATION OF FAITH* ———

I have been called by God to fulfill the destiny that He has for my life. He has made me great and has blessed me with an abundance of all good things. All of my needs and desires are fully met in Him.

If I honor God, He has promised to promote me to a position of prominence.

I am blessed and I am a blessing. In this awesome prosperity that I enjoy from my heavenly Father, I have plenty for myself, with an abundance left over so that I can be a blessing to others.

God blesses those who bless me and curses those who curse me.

He brings me to the place of abundant favors and confers on me happiness and prosperity.

(Jeremiah 29:11; Hebrews 12:1-3; 2 Corinthians 9:8,9; Exodus 23:20-22; Psalm 23)

GENESIS 13:2 KJV

Abram was very rich in cattle, in silver, and in gold.

——— *DECLARATION OF FAITH* ———

I am blessed just like Abraham because I serve the same God. My God is my Provider and He lacks nothing. He is a God of abundance who rejoices in my prosperity. In Him, I have an abundance in all things.

(Genesis 30:43; 1 Corinthians 2:9; 2 Corinthians 6:10; 8:9; Deuteronomy 8:8-18; Psalm 35:27; Galatians 3:6-14)

GENESIS 15:1 AMP

After these things, the word of the Lord came to Abram in a vision, saying, Fear not, Abram, I am your Shield, your abundant compensation, and your reward shall be exceedingly great.

——— *DECLARATION OF FAITH* ———

I am afraid of nothing! God, the Creator of the universe, is my Shield. He grants me abundance to the extreme. My reward, in Him, is exceedingly great.

(2 Timothy 1:7; Joshua 1:5-9; Psalm 3:3; 5:12; Deuteronomy 28:1-14; 2 John 8)

LUKE 1:50-55 KJV

His mercy is on them that fear him from generation to generation. He hath shewed strength with his arm; he hath scattered the proud in the imagination of their hearts. He hath put down the mighty from *their* seats, and exalted them of low degree. He hath filled the hungry with good things; and the rich he hath sent empty away. He hath holpen his servant Israel, in remembrance of *his* mercy; As he spake to our fathers, to Abraham, and to his seed for ever.

———— DECLARATION OF FAITH ————

My Father's mercy and compassion never leave me. Because I have humbled myself and placed my life in His hands, He reaches out to show me His favor continually.

He performs mighty deeds on my behalf, and scatters those who are proud and haughty, and fantasize about how wonderful they are.

He brings down rulers from their thrones, but in my humility, He lifts me to the place of highest honor.

He fills and satisfies me with good things of every kind and never causes bad things to happen to me.

He lays His hand upon me to help me and He espouses my cause.

His thoughts toward me are rooted in His mercy and loving-kindness.

I have become His friend and He has become my trusted ally. Everything that He promised to Abraham and his descendants has become my inheritance.

(Psalm 33:10; 98:1-3; 103:5,13; 126:2,3; Romans 8:38,39; 1 Peter 5:5-7; Proverbs 3:3,4; Ephesians 2:6; James 4:6-10; Jeremiah 29:11; Isaiah 54:17; 1 John 2:1,2; John 15:15; Galatians 3:14,29; 2 Corinthians 1:20)

ROMANS 9:6,7 KJV

Not as though the word of God hath taken none effect. For they are not all Israel, which are of Israel: Neither, because they are the seed of Abraham, are they all children: but, In Isaac shall thy seed be called.

—— *DECLARATION OF FAITH* ——

I am a true member of the house of Israel and a descendant of Abraham, the father of my faith. I am the very offspring to whom the promise applies.

(Galatians 3:7,29; 4:23; 6:16; Ephesians 2:18; 1 John 3:1,2)

A GOOD MARRIAGE

God's promises for a good marriage are promises of guidance. They are promises that will show you what to do to produce the intended result of marital bliss. They are not magic potions. God does not promise to change your wife and make her the person you think she should be. However, He will change you and help you to love her the way she should be loved.

What God does promise is that if you give yourself in service and submission, you will sow the seeds that will create a good marriage. It takes work and selfless sacrifice. Never forget that agape love does not seek its own, but rather the good of the other. When two people go into a marriage with that attitude, only good can come of it.

A healthy marriage is a life of service, not selfishness. No one should get married unless they have found someone to whom they are willing to give their life in service.

As you pray these prayers, examine your own heart. Make the decision that you are going to do things God's way, and He will reward you openly for it.

PROVERBS 14:11 KJV

The house of the wicked shall be overthrown: but the tabernacle of the upright shall flourish.

—— *DECLARATION OF FAITH* ——

My home is stable and secure. Its foundation is immovable.

(Psalm 112; Matthew 7:24,25; 1 Corinthians 3:11)

ECCLESIASTES 4:9-12 KJV

Two are better than one; because they have a good reward for their labour. For if they fall, the one will lift up his fellow: but woe to him *that is* alone when he falleth; for *he hath* not another to help him up. Again, if two lie together, then they have heat: but how can one be warm *alone?* And if one prevail against him, two shall withstand him; and a threefold cord is not quickly broken.

——— DECLARATION OF FAITH ———

I am wise to seek godly companionship in the things that I do. I understand that two can bring in a better harvest than one, for if one of us falls, the other can lift him (or her) up. Furthermore, if one of us is overpowered, the other can step in and lend a hand so that we can withstand every foe.

I am not an island in my walk with God. I am a companion of God's children and together, with God entwined in us and through us, we will be victorious in every situation.

(Proverbs 15:22; Ephesians 5:1-18; Hebrews 10:25; Deuteronomy 32:30)

MALACHI 2:15,16 NKJV

But did He not make *them* one,
Having a remnant of the Spirit?
And why one?
He seeks godly offspring.
Therefore take heed to your spirit,
And let none deal treacherously with the wife of his youth.
"For the Lord God of Israel says
That He hates divorce,
For it covers one's garment with violence,"
Says the Lord of hosts.

"Therefore take heed to your spirit,
That you do not deal treacherously."

— *DECLARATION OF FAITH* —

I guard myself diligently in my spirit so that I may remain faithful to my spouse. Together, God has made us one flesh and we produce godly offspring. Our sons and daughters walk in holiness before the Lord.

I will not disgrace myself by being violent to my spouse in any way, nor will I use divorce as a solution for non-reconciled differences.

I hold these principles as sacred and guard myself diligently in my spirit so that I will not break faith.

(Genesis 2:24; Ephesians 5:22-6:4; Matthew 19:4-12;
1 Corinthians 7:14)

MATTHEW 19:4-6 KJV

He answered and said unto them, Have ye not read, that he which made *them* at the beginning made them male and female, and said, For this cause shall a man leave father and mother, and shall cleave to his wife: and they twain shall be one flesh? Wherefore they are no more twain, but one flesh. What therefore God hath joined together, let not man put asunder.

— DECLARATION OF FAITH —

I have become one with my wife. God himself has joined us together and we are no longer two, but one flesh. We are united firmly and joined inseparably in a marital covenant sealed with the blood of Jesus. The bonding agent that holds us together is the very Holy Spirit himself.

Though I honor my parents, I am no longer tied to them. I always maintain proper priorities. I serve God first, my wife second, and my family third.

(Genesis 1:26,27; 2:24; Ephesians 5:22-33; 1 Corinthians 7:3,33)

EPHESIANS 5:25-33 KJV

Husbands, love your wives, even as Christ also loved the church, and gave himself for it; That he might sanctify and cleanse it with the washing of water by the word, That he might present it to himself a glorious church, not having spot, or wrinkle, or any such thing; but that it should be holy and without blemish. So ought men to love their wives as their own bodies. He that loveth his wife loveth himself. For no man ever yet hated his own flesh; but nourisheth and cherisheth it, even as the Lord the church: For we are members of his body, of his flesh, and of his bones. For this cause shall a man leave his father and mother, and shall be joined unto his wife, and they two shall be one flesh. This is a great mystery: but I speak concerning Christ and the church. Nevertheless let every one of you in particular so love his wife even as himself; and the wife see that she reverence her husband.

———— DECLARATION OF FAITH ————

I will love my wife just as Christ loved the church and gave Himself for her in order to make her holy, and cleanse her by the washing of water through the Word, and to present her to Himself as radiant, without spot or stain or any other blemish—holy and blameless.

I give myself wholly to my wife. I will love her as I do my own body. As I love myself, so I will love her. I will make no demands of her, but that love be the center of our lives. And I will be of service to her, providing for her every need just as Christ does the church.

It is written, "For this reason a man will leave his father and mother and be united to his wife, and the two will become one flesh." This is a type of Christ and the church. Just as I have become one with Christ, I have become one with my wife. Therefore, I will love my wife just as I love my own body.

(Colossians 1:22; 3:19; John 15:3,12,13; 17:17; Hebrews 10:22; Genesis 2:23,24; 1 Corinthians 6:16; 7:3,4; Proverbs 18:22)

TO MAKE YOU A GOOD PARENT

As Dr. Dobson (popular author and founder of Focus on the Family) says, "Parenting isn't for cowards!" We have to be willing to make the tough decisions and display tough love when necessary. We need to set the boundaries for our children and stick to our guns no matter how much it hurts. Discipline is utterly essential if we want our children to live good and wholesome lives. However, discipline is a secondary thing in the role of a good parent.

The Word says to train our children in the nurture and admonition of the Lord. (Eph. 6:4.) Notice that nurture comes first. If we show our children love, spend time with them, become involved in what they are doing, and teach them with a heart of compassion, we will eliminate most of the need to discipline them.

Pray these prayers with the thought of love foremost in your mind. Make your heavenly Father your role model and raise your children the way that He raises you.

DEUTERONOMY 4:9 NKJV

"Only take heed to yourself, and diligently keep yourself, lest you forget the things your eyes have seen, and lest they depart from your heart all the days of your life. And teach them to your children and your grandchildren."

—— *DECLARATION OF FAITH* ——

I attend and give my complete attention to all that the Lord has done for me. I do not let it slip from my mind. I keep these things in the midst of my heart all the days of my life. I will teach them to my children and my grandchildren as long as I have breath within me.

(Deuteronomy 6:4-12; 8:19; 29:2-8; Genesis 18:9;
Psalm 103:18; 119:11)

DEUTERONOMY 6:5-13 KJV

Thou shalt love the Lord thy God with all thine heart, and with all thy soul, and with all thy might. And these words, which I command thee this day, shall be in thine heart: And thou shalt teach them diligently unto thy children, and shalt talk of them when thou sittest in thine house, and when thou walkest by the way, and when thou liest down, and when thou risest up. And thou shalt bind them for a sign upon thine hand, and they shall be as frontlets between thine eyes. And thou shalt write them upon the posts of thy house, and on thy gates. And it shall be, when the Lord thy God shall have brought thee into the land which he sware unto thy fathers, to Abraham, to Isaac, and to Jacob, to give thee great and goodly cities, which thou buildedst not, and houses full of all good *things,* which thou filledst not, and wells digged, which thou diggedst not, vineyards and olive trees, which thou plantedst not; when thou shalt have eaten and be full; *Then* beware lest thou forget the Lord, which brought thee forth out of the land of Egypt, from the house of bondage. Thou shalt fear the Lord thy God, and serve him, and shalt swear by his name.

DECLARATION OF FAITH

I love my heavenly Father with all of my mind, all of my spirit, and all of my physical strength.

His Word is implanted and deeply rooted in my mind and in my heart.

I whet and sharpen the Word within me that it may pierce through to my mind and my spirit.

I impress the statutes of my God diligently upon the minds of my children. I talk of them when I sit in my house, when I walk by the wayside, when I lie down and when I rise up. I bind them as a sign on my hand and as an ornament before my eyes. I write them on the door-posts of my house and upon my gates.

By these statutes I receive an abundance of blessings.

By the promise of the Lord, I am brought into a prosperous dwelling. Through Him, my home is supplied with an abundance of good things.

All that I have has been given to me by His grace.

It is the Lord who prospers me and gives me an inheritance of things that I did not provide.

I will not forget what He has done for me.

(Deuteronomy 4:29; 8:6-18; Ephesians 3:17; Mark 4:13-20; Psalm 112:1-3; Romans 5:1,2,17; 8:14-17; Philippians 4:19)

JOSHUA 24:15-18 KJV

If it seem evil unto you to serve the Lord, choose you this day whom ye will serve; whether the gods which your fathers served that *were* on the other side of the flood, or the gods of the Amorites, in whose land ye dwell: but as for me and my house, we will serve the Lord. And the people answered and said, God forbid that we should forsake the Lord, to serve other gods; For the Lord our God, he *it is* that brought us up and our fathers out of the land of Egypt, from the house of bondage, and which did those great signs in our sight, and preserved us in all the way wherein we went, and among all the people through whom we passed: And the Lord drave out from before us all the people, even the Amorites which dwelt in the land: *therefore* will we also serve the Lord; for he *is* our God.

———— *DECLARATION OF FAITH* ————

As for me and my house, we will serve the Lord.

Far be it from me to forsake my Father who paid such an awesome price to recreate me in this way.

He brought me out of the land of slavery and from the house of bondage.

He has done great signs and wonders on my behalf and I will not forget it.

(1 Kings 18:21; Psalm 116:16; Exodus 23:24,25; Acts 4:23-31; Colossians 1:13; Luke 4:18)

PROVERBS 19:18 NIV

Discipline your son, for in that there is hope; do not be a willing party to his death.

———— *DECLARATION OF FAITH* ————

I render my children consistent and godly discipline. By this, I give them hope and ensure them a stable future. I refuse to be a party to their destruction, either by

*restraining from the rod, or by giving it too harshly and
without good reason.*

(Proverbs 13:24; 22:6; Ephesians 6:4)

PROVERBS 22:6 NIV

Train a child in the way he should go, and when he is old
he will not turn from it.

— *DECLARATION OF FAITH* —

*I consistently train my children in the ways of right-
eousness. I hold them to the ways of the Lord, so that
when they move out on their own, they will be stout
against temptation and have the tools to live a blessed
and prosperous life.*

(Ephesians 6:4; 2 Timothy 3:15; Deuteronomy 6:5-7)

TO CARE FOR YOUR CHILDREN

When your children suffer, you suffer with them. You hurt every time they hurt. With every tear they shed, you shed one with them. You want all that is best for them, and you do everything you can to see that they get it.

God knows your heart, Dad. He is the One who placed such a caring spirit within you. Psalm 103:13 tells us that as a loving father cares for his children, so does the Lord care for you. You can know today that God loves your kids dearly and will care for them relentlessly. Read these promises and be comforted; your heavenly Father has made His promise, and He will not let you down. His hands shall surround your children now and forevermore.

Ezra 8:21-23 KJV

Then I proclaimed a fast there, at the river of Ahava, that we might afflict ourselves before our God, to seek of him a right way for us, and for our little ones, and for all our substance. For I was ashamed to require of the king a band of soldiers and horsemen to help us against the enemy in the way: because we had spoken unto the king, saying, The hand of our God *is* upon all them for good that seek him; but his power and his wrath *is* against all them that forsake him. So we fasted and besought our God for this: and he was intreated of us.

─────── *DECLARATION OF FAITH* ───────

I look to God alone as my safeguard from trouble. He protects my family and me in all circumstances and in every situation. My children dwell in safety within His powerful arms. He takes special care to guard all of those who are with me and sees to it that the enemy does not plunder us.

The Lord answers my every prayer. His gracious hand is upon me because I look to Him alone as my shield.

(Ezra 7:6; Psalm 5:11,12; 23; 33:18,19; Genesis 15:1; Romans 8:28; Malachi 3:11)

PSALM 128:1-4 NKJV

Blessed is every one who fears the Lord, who walks in His ways. When you eat the labor of your hands, you shall be happy, and it shall be well with you. Your wife shall be like a fruitful vine in the very heart of your house, your children like olive plants all around your table. Behold, thus shall the man be blessed who fears the Lord.

——— *DECLARATION OF FAITH* ———

I walk in the ways of almighty God as a good son and disciple. I mimic His ways. In every way possible, I live like God lives.

I eat the fruit of my labor and live my life in happiness, peace, divine favor, and good fortune of every kind.

My wife is fruitful and productive within my house, and my children are anointed and blessed at my table.

My life is a pleasure to live.

(Ephesians 5:1; John 10:10; Ecclesiastes 2:24; 3:22; Psalm 52:8; 144:12; 127:3-5; Proverbs 31:10-31; 1 Peter 3:10,11)

ISAIAH 44:1-5 KJV

Yet now hear, O Jacob my servant; and Israel, whom I have chosen: Thus saith the Lord that made thee, and formed thee from the womb, *which* will help thee; Fear not, O Jacob, my servant; and thou, Jesurun, whom I have chosen. For I will pour water upon him that is thirsty, and floods upon the dry ground: I will pour my spirit upon thy seed, and my blessing upon thine offspring: And they shall spring up *as* among the grass, as willows by the water courses. One shall say, I *am* the Lord's; and another shall call *himself* by the name of Jacob; and another shall subscribe *with* his hand unto the Lord, and surname *himself* by the name of Israel.

DECLARATION OF FAITH

I have been chosen by God to be His own son. He actually picked me to be a part of His family. He has recreated me in righteousness and helps me in every area of my life. He proclaims His blessing on all that I have and prospers all that I set my hand to do.

God has given me His Word that He will pour out His Spirit and His blessings on my children. They spring up like grass in a meadow—like poplar trees by flowing streams. Their life force is full of health, energy, and vitality. They never go hungry or parched. Each of them is grafted into God's family, taking the name of the Lord as their very own.

(John 15:16-19; Psalm 103:17; Genesis 12:1-3; Deuteronomy 28:12; Acts 11:14; Ephesians 3:15)

ISAIAH 54:13-17 KJV

All thy children *shall be* taught of the Lord; and great *shall be* the peace of thy children. In righteousness shalt thou be established: thou shalt be far from oppression; for thou shalt not fear: and from terror; for it shall not come near thee. Behold, they shall surely gather together, *but* not by me: whosoever shall gather together against thee shall fall for thy sake. Behold, I have created the smith that bloweth the coals in the fire, and that bringeth forth an instrument for his work; and I have created the waster to destroy. No weapon that is formed against thee shall prosper; and every tongue *that* shall rise against thee in judgment thou shalt condemn. This *is* the heritage of the servants of the Lord, and their righteousness *is* of me, saith the Lord.

—— *DECLARATION OF FAITH* ——

My children are taught by the Lord and He gives them tremendous peace and security.

My household is established in righteousness before Him and tyranny cannot gain a foothold in my life.

I have complete authority over all fear, anxiety, stress, and terror. I will not permit them in my life in any shape or form.

If I come under attack in any way, I know it is not the Lord's doing. All of His actions toward me are for good and never evil. It is He who gives me strength to conquer the enemy. Because of this, no weapon formed against me can prevail over me and I thwart every accusation that comes against me.

This is part of my inheritance as God's son, and my righteousness and justification come from Him.

(Psalm 89:3,4; Jeremiah 29:11; 2 Timothy 1:7; Romans 5:1,2; 8:31,32,37)

ISAIAH 61:6-10 KJV

Ye shall be named the Priests of the Lord: *men* shall call you the Ministers of our God: ye shall eat the riches of the Gentiles, and in their glory shall ye boast yourselves. For your shame *ye shall have* double; and *for* confusion they shall rejoice in their portion: therefore in their land they shall possess the double: everlasting joy shall be unto them. For I the Lord love judgment, I hate robbery for burnt offering; and I will direct their work in truth, and I will make an everlasting covenant with them. And their seed shall be known among the Gentiles, and their offspring among the people: all that see them shall acknowledge them, that they *are* the seed *which* the Lord hath blessed. I will greatly rejoice in the Lord, my soul shall be joyful in my God; for he hath clothed me with the garments of salvation, he hath covered me with the robe of

righteousness, as a bridegroom decketh *himself* with orna-
ments, and as a bride adorneth *herself* with her jewels.

─────── *DECLARATION OF FAITH* ───────

    *I am known as a priest of the Lord and a minister of
God's power and grace. Instead of shame, I have received
double honor; instead of confusion and disgrace, I leap
for joy in the presence of my Father, for He has given me
a double portion for my inheritance. In His faithfulness,
He has honored His everlasting covenant with me and
has granted me a tremendous reward.*

    *My children are blessed because of the covenant.
They shall enjoy the richness of God's inheritance with
me. All who see me will acknowledge that I am a man
whom God has blessed.*

    *I delight in all of these things. My soul rejoices
within me and my spirit pays homage to my Lord and
Father, for He has clothed me with the garments of salvation and arrayed me in a robe of His righteousness.*

(Revelation 1:6; 2 Corinthians 5:20; Job 42:10-12;
Psalm 103:17; 112; Deuteronomy 28:1-14)

WISDOM

God is wisdom, and He gives wisdom, knowledge, and understanding to those who reverence Him. (Prov. 2:6.) If you have a deep, reverential sense of trust and accountability to Him, then you are on the springboard of all wisdom. That means you know that God is great and awesome in power and majesty. You know that He is faithful and true and is worthy of all praise and adoration.

It means that you have decided to take Him at His Word no matter what the circumstances look like. It means that you know and accept that His knowledge is vastly superior to yours, and He knows what needs to be done much more than you do. You know that His Word makes you wiser than your enemies, and even the teachers and philosophers that the world so admires.

You never say such foolish words as, "I know God promised that, *but....*" You are a child of the God of all wisdom, and you trust your heavenly Father regardless of what your eyes see, your ears hear, or what is going on around you. You trust Him and receive His wisdom willingly. You know beyond any shadow of doubt that He is causing you to walk in that wisdom every day of your life.

1 CHRONICLES 22:12,13 KJV

Only the Lord give thee wisdom and understanding, and give thee charge concerning Israel, that thou mayest keep the law of the Lord thy God. Then shalt thou prosper, if thou takest heed to fulfil the statutes and judgments which the Lord charged Moses with concerning Israel: be strong, and of good courage; dread not, nor be dismayed.

─── DECLARATION OF FAITH ───

I am a child of wisdom and understanding. I have been anointed with an abundance of wisdom so that I may be greatly successful in my calling.

Everything that I set my hand to do prospers and is brought to unfailing success.

I refuse to give in to fear and doubt. I am not dismayed. I am strong and of good courage, for the Lord is always with me to shield me and give me the victory.

(1 Corinthians 1:30: 2:6-16; 15:57; Daniel 1:17,20; Deuteronomy 28:12; Genesis 39:2-5; James 1:5-8; Joshua 1:5-9)

Proverbs 2:3-8 kjv

Yea, if thou criest after knowledge, *and* liftest up thy voice for understanding; If thou seekest her as silver, and searchest for her as *for* hid treasures; Then shalt thou understand the fear of the Lord, and find the knowledge of God. For the Lord giveth wisdom: out of his mouth *cometh* knowledge and understanding. He layeth up sound wisdom for the righteous: *he is* a buckler to them that walk uprightly. He keepeth the paths of judgment, and preserveth the way of his saints.

— DECLARATION OF FAITH —

The search for wisdom is of prime importance in my life. For me, it is like searching for a great hidden treasure, for I know that when I find it, I will understand the fear of the Lord and gain personal and intimate knowledge of God. It is the Lord's good will to grant me wisdom; therefore, I know that when I seek it out, He will make certain that I find it.

Through God's Word, I gain tremendous knowledge and understanding.

He holds victory in reserve for me and stands guard with me in every circumstance and endeavor that I undertake.

(1 Corinthians 1:30; 2:6-16; 15:57; Proverbs 3:14; James 1:5,6; 1 Kings 3:9-12)

ISAIAH 33:5,6 AMP

The Lord is exalted, for He dwells on high; He will fill Zion with justice and righteousness (moral and spiritual rectitude in every area and relation). And there shall be stability in your times, an abundance of salvation, wisdom, and knowledge; the reverent fear and worship of the Lord is your treasure and His.

——— *DECLARATION OF FAITH* ———

I trust in the Lord with all of my heart and He fills me with His justice and righteousness. He is the sure foundation of my life and my stability in every situation. Out of His abundance, He brings me a full supply of wisdom, knowledge, and salvation for every circumstance that I face. As His son, I have free access to all of His treasures.

(Proverbs 3:5-10; 1 Corinthians 1:30; 2:6-16; Romans 5:17; 8:16-21,32; Galatians 4:5)

ACTS 7:22 AMP

So Moses was educated in all the wisdom and culture of the Egyptians, and he was mighty (powerful) in his speech and deeds.

I have a tremendous aspiration for learning the knowledge and wisdom of this present world. By this, I stand mighty in speech and deeds in the eyes of the world and thus become of even greater use to the Lord.

(Daniel 1:4,17,20; 2:22,23; 2 Corinthians 1:30; 2:6-16; 14:2,13; Luke 24:19)

JAMES 3:13-18 KJV

Who *is* a wise man and endued with knowledge among you? let him shew out of a good conversation his works with meekness of wisdom. But if ye have bitter envying and strife in your hearts, glory not, and lie not against the truth. This wisdom descendeth not from above, but *is* earthly, sensual, devilish. For where envying and strife *is,* there *is* confusion and every evil work. But the wisdom that is from above is first pure, then peaceable, gentle, *and* easy to be intreated, full of mercy and good fruits, without partiality, and without hypocrisy. And the fruit of righteousness is sown in peace of them that make peace.

———— *DECLARATION OF FAITH* ————

I am a man of wisdom and understanding. This I freely display by living a good and upright life—by deeds done in the humility that comes from wisdom.

I refuse to harbor bitter envy or selfish ambition in my heart. That kind of wisdom is devilish and I will have no part of it; for where there is envy and selfish ambition, there is disorder and evil of every kind.

My wisdom comes from heaven. It is first pure, then peace-loving, considerate, willing to yield to what is right and godly, full of mercy, impartial, sincere, and produces an abundance of good fruit.

As a peacemaker, I sow in peace and raise an abundant harvest of righteousness.

(Daniel 2:22,23; Matthew 13:11,15,16; 1 Corinthians 2:6-16; 3:2,3; 1 John 3:18; Romans 12:9-21; 13:13,14; Philippians 3:18,19; Proverbs 11:18)

GUIDANCE

In society today we have more distractions than ever that could cause us to stray from the plan that God has for our lives. This is what makes His promises of guidance so precious to us.

There are many ways in which God promises guidance. He guides through His Word, through the fellowship of the Holy Spirit, through pastors and ministers, and sometimes even through the words of children. God may also guide you through a flow of supernatural favor or even by placing obstacles in your path.

No matter how He chooses to guide you, you can rest assured that if you cling to His promises, you will reach the intended destination He has for you. The path may not make much sense, but His Word says that it will be plain. For His very name's sake, He will make sure that you know when you are headed in the right direction.

PSALM 25:3-5 NIV

No one whose hope is in you will ever be put to shame, but they will be put to shame who are treacherous without excuse. Show me your ways, O Lord, teach me your paths; guide me in your truth and teach me, for you are God my Savior, and my hope is in you all day long.

——— *DECLARATION OF FAITH* ———

I will never be put to shame for trusting in the Lord. He shows me His ways and teaches me His paths so that I have a full understanding of His will for my life. He guides me in His truth and reveals to me all that I need to know to reign as a king in this life. My hope is in Him every second, of every minute, of every hour, of every day.

(Romans 1:16; 5:17; 1 Corinthians 2:6-16; Exodus 33:13; Psalm 5:8-12; 86:11)

PSALM 25:9-15 KJV

The meek will he guide in judgment: and the meek will he teach his way. All the paths of the Lord are mercy and truth unto such as keep his covenant and his testimonies. For thy name's sake, O Lord, pardon mine iniquity; for it is great. What man is he that feareth the Lord? him shall he teach in the way that he shall choose. His soul shall dwell at ease; and his seed shall inherit the earth. The secret of the Lord is with them that fear him; and he will shew them his covenant. Mine eyes are ever toward the Lord; for he shall pluck my feet out of the net.

── DECLARATION OF FAITH ──

I humble myself under God's mighty hand and He guides me in the ways of righteousness. He teaches me His ways so that I have an intimate understanding of His will.

I have a thorough understanding of His love and faithfulness toward me. He is not good to me only some of the time, He is good to me all of the time.

I am His covenant partner and a child who bears His name.

He has forgiven my every iniquity and washed away even the worst of my stains. He has chosen a path for me to walk in and guides me in it without fail.

His desire for me is prosperity—a life full of riches and an abundance of all good things.

He has declared that my descendants will inherit the land.

I will never take my eyes off of Him, for He is my only hope of freedom from the invisible snares of the devil.

(1 Peter 5:5-7; 1 Corinthians 2:6-16; Psalm 27:11; 69:35,36; 91:3; 103:1-5; 143:11; John 10:10; 15:15; Leviticus 26:9; Hebrews 8:6; 10:15-17; Genesis 50:20)

PSALM 119:105-107 NKJV

Your word is a lamp to my feet and a light to my path. I have sworn and confirmed that I will keep Your righteous judgments. I am afflicted very much; revive me, O Lord, according to Your word.

————— *DECLARATION OF FAITH* —————

God's Word is a lamp unto my feet and a light unto my path.

I have taken my oath, and confirmed it with deeds tried and true, that I will follow the precepts that my Father has laid out for me.

Therefore, I shall remain in good health and my vitality shall be preserved until I have lived a long, happy, and prosperous life.

(Proverbs 6:23; Nehemiah 10:29; 1 John 3:18; Isaiah 46:4; Psalm 107:20)

ISAIAH 42:16 NKJV

I will bring the blind by a way they did not know; I will lead them in paths they have not known. I will make darkness light before them, and crooked places straight. These things I will do for them, and not forsake them.

————— *DECLARATION OF FAITH* —————

The Holy Spirit is always with me to guide and direct me on the path of life. He turns the darkness into light before me and makes the rough places smooth. I have His Word that He will do this and that He will never leave me nor forsake me.

(John 16:13; Psalm 119:105; Isaiah 30:21; Hebrews 13:5,6)

EZEKIEL 1:12 NIV

Each one went straight ahead. Wherever the spirit would go, they would go, without turning as they went.

——— *DECLARATION OF FAITH* ———

I am led by the Spirit of God. Wherever He goes, I go. I cannot be diverted from the path that He has set before me.

(Romans 8:14; John 16:13; Deuteronomy 28:14)

SUCCESS

What is true success? Is it measured in the size of your bank account, the title you have, or the level of your education? All of these may define certain levels of success, but true success is simply being the person you were created to be.

You are a son of the kingdom of God with a specific God-given mission and purpose in life. If you are fulfilling that purpose, then God's kingdom is advancing, and He will see to it that you also have other necessities and luxuries of life as well.

If you believe that acquiring wealth is what brings you success, then you are probably going through a lot of unnecessary hardships. On the other hand, if you are seeking the prosperity and advancement of God's kingdom first, you will be worry free, and God will take care of the wealth for you. The key, again, is simply being the person you were created to be.

GENESIS 39:2-5 KJV

The Lord was with Joseph, and he was a prosperous man; and he was in the house of his master the

Egyptian. And his master saw that the Lord was with him, and that the Lord made all that he did to prosper in his hand. And Joseph found grace in his sight, and he served him: and he made him overseer over his house, and all that he had put into his hand. And it came to pass from the time that he had made him overseer in his house, and over all that he had, that the Lord blessed the Egyptian's house for Joseph's sake; and the blessing of the Lord was upon all that he had in the house, and in the field.

——— *DECLARATION OF FAITH* ———

The Lord is always with me to make me prosperous and very successful.

Those who have been appointed as my supervisors can clearly see that the Lord is with me. They see how He makes everything that I set my hand to do to thrive and prosper.

He grants me abundant favor with those in authority over me. They look upon me as one who is called to lead and the Lord blesses them for my sake. For my sake, all that they have is blessed.

(Genesis 30:29,30; Deuteronomy 8:6-18; 28:1-14; Daniel 1:20; Acts 7:9,10)

NEHEMIAH 2:20 AMP

I answered them, The God of heaven will prosper us; therefore we His servants will arise and build, but you have no portion or right or memorial in Jerusalem.

——— *DECLARATION OF FAITH* ———

My Father grants me success in all that I set my hand to do. He bids me to lay claim to my rightful inheritance in this earth.

(Genesis 39:2-5; Deuteronomy 28:12; Joshua 1:8; Galatians 4:5,6; Romans 8:17)

JOB 36:7-11 KJV

He withdraweth not his eyes from the righteous: but with kings *are they* on the throne; yea, he doth establish them for ever, and they are exalted. And if *they be* bound in fetters, *and* be holden in cords of affliction; Then he sheweth them their work, and their transgressions that they have exceeded. He openeth also their ear to discipline, and commandeth that they return from iniquity. If they obey and serve *him*, they shall spend their days in prosperity, and their years in pleasures.

— DECLARATION OF FAITH —

The Lord's eyes never leave me. He keeps watch over all that I do and is my ever-present help to ensure my success.

He corrects and disciplines me when I waiver and makes sure that I know what I have done wrong. He then sets me back on the path of His prosperity and sees to it that I spend my days in peace and contentment.

(Nehemiah 1:5,6; Psalm 33:18; 34:15; 46:1; 91:15,16; Hebrews 12:1-16; 13:5,6; Joel 2:25,26)

PSALM 118:5-17 KJV

I called upon the Lord in distress: the Lord answered me, *and set me* in a large place. The Lord *is* on my side; I will not fear: what can man do unto me? The Lord taketh my part with them that help me: therefore shall I see *my desire* upon them that hate me. *It is* better to trust in the Lord than to put confidence in man. *It is* better to trust in the Lord than to put confidence in princes. All nations compassed me about: but in the name of the Lord will I destroy them. They compassed me about; yea, they compassed me about: but in the name of the Lord I will destroy them. They compassed me about like bees; they are quenched as the fire of thorns: for in the name of the Lord I will destroy them. Thou hast thrust sore at me that I might fall: but the Lord helped me. The Lord *is* my strength and song, and is become my salvation. The voice of rejoicing and salvation *is* in the tabernacles of the righteous: the right hand of the Lord doeth valiantly. The right hand of the Lord is exalted: the right hand of the Lord doeth valiantly. I shall not die, but live, and declare the works of the Lord.

DECLARATION OF FAITH

When I was alone and without help, I cried out to God. I knew in my heart that only He could save me and deliver me from Satan's bondage. And faithful to His Word, He set me free. He dashed to pieces the chains that bound me and made me a prince in His royal family.

He is now with me at all times and is totally devoted to my success in this life.

I have no fear when men try to destroy me, for I know that God is on my side. To be afraid would be utterly foolish—just as it is foolish to come against one of God's children.

I have the complete and unqualified certainty that victory is mine.

I would much rather take my refuge in the Lord than to trust in the ways of men. Even the princes of this earth are paupers compared to the ones who are in alliance with God.

All I need to do is lift up the name of Jesus in my defense and they are thwarted.

Even when I stumble in battle, the Lord lifts me up. He is always with me and He never stumbles. He is my strength, my song, and my continual salvation. Shouts of victory are constantly heard in my house, for the Lord is a mighty God and has done great things on my behalf!

(Ephesians 2:1-10; John 3:16,17; Colossians 1:13,14;
Hebrews 13:5,6; 1 Corinthians 15:57; Romans 8:31; 12:9-21;
2 Timothy 1:7; 2:13; Genesis 12:3; 2 Chronicles 32:7;
2 Kings 6:15-17; Psalm 35:4; 54:4; 59:10; 88:17; 146:3)

DANIEL 5:29 NIV

Then at Belshazzar's command, Daniel was clothed in purple, a gold chain was placed around his neck, and he was proclaimed the third highest ruler in the kingdom.

——— *DECLARATION OF FAITH* ———

I am honored for my faithfulness in God's kingdom. Rulers shower me with gifts and award me with positions of honor and leadership.

(Deuteronomy 28:1-14; Genesis 39:2-5,21; 41:37-45; Job 29;
Proverbs 3:3,4)

EMPLOYMENT

Did you know that it is your right as a son of God to have a satisfying and fulfilling career? It is actually a part of the inheritance that your Father has left for you. If you think about it, it is only logical. God did not create you with specific gifts and talents in order to put you in a career where you never get to use them. Furthermore, God wants you to be happy.

Everyone looks forward to doing those things that they are gifted to do. It is what we are best at; and when we do them, we can make the most difference in the lives of others. Therefore, we can know that the career that God designed us for will bring us joy, satisfaction, and fulfillment.

Take inventory of yourself. Is what you are doing in life making you miserable? Can you say that what you are doing is what God created you for? If not, seek His guidance. I promise you He will open the eyes of your understanding and give you a revelation of His purpose for your life. As for now, do the very best you can where you are and God will open up a flow of favor that will lead you into the place He intends for you to be.

1 CHRONICLES 15:22 AMP

Chenaniah, leader of the Levites in singing, was put in charge of carrying the ark and lifting up song. He instructed about these matters because he was skilled and able.

DECLARATION OF FAITH

I am skilled in what God has called me to do. He has anointed me with great expertise on the job and in the work of the kingdom. In all matters that I am faced with, I am competent and well able to perform extraordinarily well.

(Daniel 1:17,20; 2:22,23; Ecclesiastes 3:22; Genesis 39:2-5; 1 John 2:20; Philippians 2:12,13; 1 Corinthians 2:6-16)

PROVERBS 22:29 AMP

Do you see a man diligent and skillful in his business? He will stand before kings; he will not stand before obscure men.

———— DECLARATION OF FAITH ————

I am diligent in my business. I am a hard worker who constantly finds ways to make things better. In my diligence I have earned the right to stand in the presence of kings. Mediocre men will find no peer in me.

(Proverbs 10:4; 12:24; 30:28; Psalm 119:146)

ECCLESIASTES 2:24-26 NIV

A man can do nothing better than to eat and drink and find satisfaction in his work. This too, I see, is from the hand of God, for without him, who can eat or find enjoyment? To the man who pleases him, God gives wisdom, knowledge and happiness, but to the sinner he gives the task of gathering and storing up wealth to hand it over to the one who pleases God. This too is meaningless, a chasing after the wind.

———— DECLARATION OF FAITH ————

I reap the benefits of my labor and find great satisfaction in my work.

I take the time to enjoy the blessings of prosperity that God has provided for me.

God has given me wisdom, knowledge, and happiness. In Him, I have a clever and resourceful mind.

(Ecclesiastes 3:12,13,22; 5:10,18-20; 8:15; 9:9;
1 Corinthians 1:30; 2:6-16; Proverbs 13:22)

EPHESIANS 6:5-8 KJV

Servants, be obedient to them that are *your* masters according to the flesh, with fear and trembling, in singleness of your heart, as unto Christ; Not with eyeservice, as menpleasers; but as the servants of Christ, doing the will of God from the heart; With good will doing service, as to the Lord, and not to men: Knowing that whatsoever good thing any man doeth, the same shall he receive of the Lord, whether *he be* bond or free.

—— *DECLARATION OF FAITH* ——

I am obedient to those who are appointed in authority over me, having respect for them and being eager to please them on the job. I am a hard worker and do my best for them, not only while they are in my presence, but at all times. I work for them as if I were serving Jesus himself, doing the will of God from my heart. I know that the good that I am doing does not go unnoticed. God sees it all and has promised me a tremendous reward. I will not forget that my heavenly Father prospers what I set my hand to do and He blesses my employers on account of me.

(Genesis 39:2-5; Colossians 3:17,22-25; 1 Timothy 6:1,2; Deuteronomy 28:12,13; 2 Chronicles 7:15)

1 PETER 2:18,19 AMP

[You who are] household servants, be submissive to your masters with all [proper] respect, not only to those who are kind and considerate and reasonable, but also to those who are surly (overbearing, unjust, and crooked). For one is regarded favorably (is approved, acceptable, and thankworthy) if, as in the sight of God, he endures the pain of unjust suffering.

——— *DECLARATION OF FAITH* ———

I submit myself to my employer with all honor, integrity, and respect. I bear up under the pain of unjust suffering because I am God-inside minded. I know that He will see me through to victory no matter what my situation may be.

(Ephesians 6:5-8; Matthew 5:10-12; 1 Peter 2:20-23)

UNIQUE ABILITIES

Too many of God's men believe that they are not as gifted as others. That is so untrue. God formed you for a specific purpose. You were born into the kingdom for such a time as this. No one can perform your purpose as well as you can. It is what you were created for. How many times have you watched others perform a function and you knew that you could do it so much better? You knew this because of the unique gifts that God has given you.

My brother, do you know that you are exceptional, one of a kind, and irreplaceable? If you do not fulfill your function, all of us will have to settle for less than the best.

Read these promises and take inventory of your talents. Take notice of those things that drive you with passion. Recognize what satisfies you and brings you joy. Do not compare yourself to others. Don't try to be what someone else is. Look within yourself. God created you for a purpose, and He placed within you every ability to fulfill that purpose. This is why we need you so much, my brother. None of us can do what you are called to do.

EXODUS 35:34,35 KJV

He hath put in his heart that he may teach, *both* he, and Aholiab, the son of Ahisamach, of the tribe of Dan. Them hath he filled with wisdom of heart, to work all manner of work, of the engraver, and of the cunning workman, and of the embroiderer, in blue, and in purple, in scarlet, and in fine linen, and of the weaver, *even* of them that do any work, and of those that devise cunning work.

——— DECLARATION OF FAITH ———

God has given me supernatural ability to teach. He has filled me with all wisdom and ability to do what He has called me to do. [And He has called me to do great things in the earth.]

(Daniel 1:17,20; 1 Corinthians 1:30; 2:10-16; 2 Timothy 2:7; Philippians 1:6; 2:13)

1 SAMUEL 16:18 NIV

One of the servants answered, "I have seen a son of Jesse of Bethlehem who knows how to play the harp. He is a brave man and a warrior. He speaks well and is a fine-looking man. And the Lord is with him."

—— *DECLARATION OF FAITH* ——

The very Spirit of God has taken up residence within me. He has empowered me to be skillful in everything that I set my hand to do. He gives me extraordinary ability to perform the duties of my profession. In a spirit of excellence, He causes me to stand out from the rest of the world.

He has made me brave, courageous, and valiant. I am intrepid in danger.

He has given me power to express myself clearly and appropriately in influential and impressive speech. I am an engaging and attractive personality, for the Lord dwells in my heart and manifests His character both in and through me.

(Ephesians 5:18; Daniel 1:17,20; Genesis 39:2-5; Joshua 1:5-9; Acts 6:10; 1 John 3:24)

1 KINGS 4:32-34 NKJV

He spoke three thousand proverbs, and his songs were one thousand and five. Also he spoke of trees, from the cedar tree of Lebanon even to the hyssop that springs out of the wall; he spoke also of animals, of birds, of creeping things, and of fish. And men of all nations, from all the kings of the earth who had heard of his wisdom, came to hear the wisdom of Solomon.

———— *DECLARATION OF FAITH* ————

I am creative and innovative.

I do not need to mimic what others have done but to have the creative ability within me to come up with new things to bless the world.

I have a thorough understanding of my surroundings and I am an innovator and inventor of what is unknown in the earth.

My Father has given me tremendous insight into the workings of all of His creation.

(Daniel 1:17,20; 2:22,23; Ecclesiastes 12:9; 1 Corinthians 1:30; 2:6-16; 2 Corinthians 5:17-21)

2 Corinthians 10:12 NKJV

We dare not class ourselves or compare ourselves with those who commend themselves. But they, measuring themselves by themselves, and comparing themselves among themselves, are not wise.

—— DECLARATION OF FAITH ——

I do not measure myself, or my ability, by what I know I can do in and of myself. I always remember that the unlimited One dwells within me, and with Him, nothing is impossible.

(John 14:12,17; 17:20-26; 2 Corinthians 5:12)

2 TIMOTHY 1:6-10 KJV

Wherefore I put thee in remembrance that thou stir up the gift of God, which is in thee by the putting on of my hands. For God hath not given us the spirit of fear; but of power, and of love, and of a sound mind. Be not thou therefore ashamed of the testimony of our Lord, nor of me his prisoner: but be thou partaker of the afflictions of the gospel according to the power of God; Who hath saved us, and called *us* with an holy calling, not according to our works, but according to his own purpose and grace, which was given us in Christ Jesus before the world began, But is now made manifest by the appearing of our Saviour Jesus Christ, who hath abolished death, and hath brought life and immortality to light through the gospel.

—— DECLARATION OF FAITH ——

I recognize that it is my responsibility to fan into flame the gift of God within me. I know that God has not given me a spirit of fear and cowardice, but of power (miraculous ability), love, and self-control. Therefore, I will remain perpetually on fire for Him, fully confident and always doing what He has called me to do.

I am not ashamed to testify about the Lord, for He has saved me and given me a holy calling, not because of anything that I have done to earn it, but because of His own purpose and grace.

According to God's sovereign plan, He chose me to receive His grace before the beginning of time. What an awesome thought it is to know that, even before the beginning of time, I held a special place in the heart of God. And now, through the appearing of my Lord and Savior Jesus Christ, who abrogated the death that was mine and brought me to life and immortality through the Gospel, that grace that was once restrained has been poured out upon me in abundance.

(Ephesians 2:1-10; 5:18; 1 Timothy 4:14; Joshua 1:5-9; Acts 1:8; Matthew 3:11,12; Romans 1:16; Titus 3:4-7; 2 Thessalonians 2:13; John 3:16)

FAVOR

Favor is God's supernatural influence, which brings you partiality and preeminence in every situation. It is the one thing that gives you an advantage over every person outside the kingdom of God. God rains His general blessings upon the just and the unjust alike, but His blessing of favor is given exclusively to His children.

Too many of us overlook the favor that God gives us. Never forget that God wants you to have all of the best things in life. Don't allow false humility to rob you of this blessing. If someone wants to do something nice for you, thank them and enjoy the favor. If someone hands you a $100 bill, thank them for it. Be appreciative of the good things done for you. It blesses the giver when you appreciate what they are doing. Don't pray for favor and then reject it when God gives it. Just be thankful and enjoy it.

EXODUS 3:21,22 AMP

I will give this people favor and respect in the sight of the Egyptians; and it shall be that when you go, you shall not go empty-handed. But every woman shall [insistently] solicit of her neighbor and of her that may be residing at her house jewels and articles of silver and gold, and garments, which you shall put on your sons and daughters; and you shall strip the Egyptians [of belongings due to you].

——— *DECLARATION OF FAITH* ———

The Lord gives me favor in the sight of my enemies. God will give me abundance where I once had lack, prosperity where I once had poverty. The enemy will be forced to give back to me all he has stolen and much, much more.

(Ephesians 6:12; Genesis 39:5; Numbers 31; Psalm 5:11,12; Proverbs 19:14; 2 Chronicles 20:15-24)

EZRA 7:9,10 NKJV

On the first *day* of the first month he began *his* journey from Babylon, and on the first *day* of the fifth month he came to Jerusalem, according to the good hand of his God upon him. For Ezra had prepared his heart to seek the Law of the Lord, and to do *it,* and to teach statutes and ordinances in Israel.

——— *DECLARATION OF FAITH* ———

I am committed to study and show myself approved unto the Lord. I will learn and observe His ways of

kingdom-living and teach them to others through both
my word and my example.

The Lord's hand of favor is upon me everywhere I go
and in everything that I do.

(2 Timothy 2:15; Nehemiah 2:18; Matthew 6:33;
Deuteronomy 4:9,10; 28:12; Genesis 39:2-5)

Ezra 8:18 NKJV

Then, by the good hand of our God upon us, they
brought us a man of understanding, of the sons of
Mahli the son of Levi, the son of Israel, namely
Sherebiah, with his sons and brothers, eighteen men.

—— *DECLARATION OF FAITH* ——

God's hand of favor is upon me in all of my endeav-
ors in life. Everything that I set my hand to do is brought
to unfailing success.

(Psalm 1:1-3; 5:11,12; Joshua 1:5-9; Deuteronomy 28:1-14;
Genesis 39:2-5)

Psalm 89:14-17 KJV

Justice and judgment *are* the habitation of thy throne:
mercy and truth shall go before thy face. Blessed *is* the
people that know the joyful sound: they shall walk, O

Lord, in the light of thy countenance. In thy name shall they rejoice all the day: and in thy righteousness shall they be exalted. For thou *art* the glory of their strength: and in thy favour our horn shall be exalted.

———— *DECLARATION OF FAITH* ————

I walk in the light of the presence of almighty God. His love and faithfulness go before me. His righteousness and justice sustain me. I have learned to acclaim His mighty name in this earth. I rejoice in Him all the day long. I am lifted up and encompassed in His righteousness. He is my glory and strength, and by His favor I am well established.

(1 John 1:3-7; Romans 8:38,39; Nehemiah 8:10; Psalm 75:10; 92:10; 132:17)

ACTS 27:3 NKJV

The next *day* we landed at Sidon. And Julius treated Paul kindly and gave *him* liberty to go to his friends and receive care.

———— *DECLARATION OF FAITH* ————

I continually walk in God's favor and people go out of their way to do nice things for me.

(Proverbs 3:3,4; Genesis 12:1-3; Exodus 3:21,22; 11:3; 12:36)

COURAGE AND
BOLDNESS

The Lord has declared that He has not given you a spirit of fear, but of power, love, and a sound mind. (2 Tim. 1:7.) Think about that. The Lord himself dwells within you. He is on your side in every circumstance that you face. What is there to be afraid of? Is He not more powerful than your enemies? Has He not told you to be strong and of good courage for He is with you wherever you go? (Deut. 31:6.) *Any* fear that comes against you is from the enemy. It is designed to rob you of your faith and make you stagnant in your walk with God.

The devil knows that if sons of God stand with courage and move forward in boldness, his strategies will be thwarted and his kingdom will fall. Therefore, I exhort you right now to be a thorn in his side. Be the fearless warrior of God that you are intended to be.

JOSHUA 1:5-9 KJV

There shall not any man be able to stand before thee all the days of thy life: as I was with Moses, *so* I will be with thee: I will not fail thee, nor forsake thee. Be strong and of a good courage: for unto this people shalt thou divide for an inheritance the land, which I sware unto their fathers to give them. Only be thou strong and very courageous, that thou mayest observe to do according to all the law, which Moses my servant commanded thee: turn not from it *to* the right hand or *to* the left, that thou mayest prosper whithersoever thou goest. This book of the law shall not depart out of thy mouth; but thou shalt meditate therein day and night, that thou mayest observe to do according to all that is written therein: for then thou shalt make thy way prosperous, and then thou shalt have good success. Have not I commanded thee? Be strong and of a good courage; be not afraid, neither be thou dismayed: for the Lord thy God *is* with thee whithersoever thou goest.

—— *DECLARATION OF FAITH* ——

Through all the days of my life, not one of my enemies will be able to stand against me.

My Father is with me. Even more so, He has taken up residence inside of me.

Therefore, I will be strong and courageous. I have complete confidence in His ability to give me the victory. I encounter danger and difficulties with firmness and without fear. I am bold, brave, and resolute. I fulfill my

*calling in a spirit of valor and determination that over-
comes any obstacle that the enemy would put in my path.*

*I do not turn from God's Word. I make it the corner-
stone of my life so that I may prosper in all that I do.*

*I speak the Word continually. I meditate upon it day
and night so that I may do all that is written therein. By
this, I make my way prosperous, have good success, and
deal wisely in all of the affairs of my life.*

*I do not shrink back from God's Word. I am faithful,
strong, vigorous, bold, and very courageous! Fear has no
place in my life, for the Lord is with me wherever I go!*

(Romans 8:31-37; Ephesians 3:16-19; Hebrew 6:12;
Deuteronomy 31:6,7; Psalm 1:1-3; Isaiah 41:10)

1 CHRONICLES 19:13 AMP

Be of good courage and let us behave ourselves courageously for our people and for the cities of our God; and
may the Lord do what is good in His sight.

—— *DECLARATION OF FAITH* ——

*I am strong and very courageous! My actions are not
birthed in fear, but in courage. I am a bold and fearless
child of the living God! I stand up courageously for my*

people! Through me, the Lord does what is good and right in this earth!

(Joshua 1:5-9; 2 Timothy 1:7; Philippians 2:12,13; 1 John 4:1-4)

PROVERBS 28:1 NKJV

The wicked flee when no one pursues,
But the righteous are bold as a lion.

——— *DECLARATION OF FAITH* ———

Worry cannot gain a foothold in my life. I maintain my focus upon my Lord and remain strong at all times. I never forget who dwells within me. I am the righteousness of God in Christ Jesus and have the courage and boldness of a lion!

(Matthew 6:19-33; Joshua 1:5-9; 1 John 4:4;
2 Corinthians 5:21; Philippians 4:4-8)

MARK 5:36 NKJV

As soon as Jesus heard the word that was spoken, He said to the ruler of the synagogue, "Do not be afraid; only believe."

——— *DECLARATION OF FAITH* ———

When I am faced with an evil report in the natural realm, I remain calm and continue to believe. I do not allow fear to rob me of what God has done for me. My faith brings to pass what I need regardless of what is seen or known in the natural world.

(Numbers 14:1-9; 2 Timothy 1:6,7; Joshua 1:5-9;
2 Corinthians 5:7; Hebrews 11:1)

ACTS 27:25 AMP

So keep up your courage, men, for I have faith (complete confidence) in God that it will be exactly as it was told me.

——— *DECLARATION OF FAITH* ———

I maintain my courage and confidence in every situation and circumstance, for I believe with all of my heart that things will go exactly as God has said.

(2 Timothy 1:6,7,12; Joshua 1:5-9; Isaiah 55:11;
Romans 4:20,21)

FAITH

So few people truly know what faith is. Here is the simplest definition I can think of: Faith is the affirmation of belief. After reading all of the Bible promises on faith, I cannot think of a better definition than that. When Paul was explaining the spirit of faith, he stated, "We too believe, and therefore we speak" (2 Cor. 4:13 AMP). James tells that faith without some corresponding action is not faith at all. It is just belief. (James 2:18-26.)

The Word also says that it is by faith and patience that we receive God's promises. (Heb. 6:12.) It does not say that we receive them by belief and patience. You do not have faith until you speak and act on it. You have to get up and do something about what you believe. Then, you cannot let circumstances cause you to doubt. You must have patience as you continue to exercise your faith. Notice I did not say as you continue to believe, but as you exercise your faith. By relentlessly continuing to affirm what you believe through your actions and words, you will inherit the promise you are believing for.

MATTHEW 13:58 KJV

He did not many mighty works there because of their unbelief.

——— *DECLARATION OF FAITH* ———

I believe in, trust in, and rely upon Jesus perpetually. His power is ever-present and at work in my life.

(1 Peter 3:12; Colossians 1:29; Ephesians 1:17-23; John 14:12)

MATTHEW 17:19,20 KJV

Then came the disciples to Jesus apart, and said, Why could not we cast him out?

And Jesus said unto them, Because of your unbelief: for verily I say unto you, If ye have faith as a grain of mustard seed, ye shall say unto this mountain, Remove hence to yonder place; and it shall remove; and nothing shall be impossible unto you.

——— *DECLARATION OF FAITH* ———

My faith is a spiritual force that is alive within me. When I use it, it is like a seed planted at the root of the problem. As I cultivate it [continually believing and speaking the answer], it overtakes and uproots whatever is standing in my way.

Even a mountain poses no difficulty for me when I remain stubborn and persistent in my faith. When I tell it to move, it moves. When I tell demons to leave, they leave.

When I command an infirmity to come out of a body, it comes out. With the faith that God has given me, nothing is impossible for me.

(2 Corinthians 4:13; John 6:63; Mark 11:22-24; Hebrews 11:1)

MARK 4:37-40 KJV

There arose a great storm of wind, and the waves beat into the ship, so that it was now full. And he was in the hinder part of the ship, asleep on a pillow: and they awake him, and say unto him, Master, carest thou not that we perish? And he arose, and rebuked the wind, and said unto the sea, Peace, be still. And the wind ceased, and there was a great calm. And he said unto them, Why are ye so fearful? how is it that ye have no faith?

—— DECLARATION OF FAITH ——

When things seem hopeless in the natural world and the storms of life are threatening, I will not be afraid. My faith has gone before me and I have God's Word that I will come to no harm. No matter what the circumstance may be, I remain secure.

*By faith, I speak to whatever situation I am facing
and command it to get in line with the perfect will of God.*

(Joshua 1:5-9; Hebrews 10:35-11:1; Psalm 91:10;
Mark 11:22-25)

LUKE 8:24,25 KJV

They came to him, and awoke him, saying, Master,
master, we perish. Then he arose, and rebuked the wind
and the raging of the water: and they ceased, and there
was a calm. And he said unto them, Where is your faith?
And they being afraid wondered, saying one to another,
What manner of man is this! for he commandeth even
the winds and water, and they obey him.

——— *DECLARATION OF FAITH* ———

I am a man of faith.

*I reject all fear and anxiety in my life, casting it all
on the shoulders of the One who bears my burdens. I am
not seized by fear in any circumstance. I have the Word
on my lips that covers and protects me in any situation.*

*I use my faith every hour of every day, believing and
speaking to the problem, commanding the circumstance
to get in line with the perfect will of God.*

I am a victor here, not a victim, and I am in command of any given situation.

(Hebrews 11:6; 1 Peter 5:5-7; 2 Timothy 1:6,7; Matthew 11:28-30; Romans 8:37; 10:8; Psalm 119:93; Joshua 1:5-9; 2 Corinthians 4:13; Mark 11:23,24)

2 CORINTHIANS 4:13 MESSAGE

Just like the psalmist who wrote, "I believed it, so I said it," we say what we believe.

— DECLARATION OF FAITH —

Faith is a spiritual power and the tool that God has given me to bring forth an abundance of good fruit in my life. It is written of the spirit of faith, "I believed; therefore, I have spoken." This is my faith in operation. I take the promise into my heart, believe it with all of my soul, and speak it forth until it is manifested in my life.

(Proverbs 18:20,21; Psalm 116:10; Hebrews 11:1,6; Mark 11:22-25; 2 Peter 1:1-4; John 6:63; Matthew 21:19-22; Romans 10:8; 2 Corinthians 5:7)

TO NEVER FAIL YOU

This ties into the category of God honoring His Word but is worthy to stand on its own. The reason I say this is because it is possible to be emotionally damaged by people who have made us promises that they never intended to keep. This is especially heartbreaking when those people who have failed us are our own parents.

God is your Father, and He doesn't want to be compared to an earthly father who doesn't really care about his child. God is good to you. He will never lie to you. You can trust Him unwaveringly, for He will never let you down.

Read these promises and take heart. God will make good on every one.

1 SAMUEL 30:6 NKJV

Now David was greatly distressed, for the people spoke of stoning him, because the soul of all the people was grieved, every man for his sons and his daughters. But David strengthened himself in the Lord his God.

—— *DECLARATION OF FAITH* ——

When turmoil comes in like a flood, I will encourage myself in the Lord. I look to God and His Word for my confidence.

When others fail me and forsake me, God takes His stand on my behalf. Together, we overcome any and every problem that I may face.

(Isaiah 25:4; 59:19; Habakkuk 3:17-19; 2 Timothy 1:6; Acts 4:23-31)

1 CHRONICLES 28:19,20 NIV

"All this," David said, "I have in writing from the hand of the Lord upon me, and he gave me understanding in all the details of the plan." David also said to Solomon his son, "Be strong and courageous, and do the work. Do not be afraid or discouraged, for the Lord God, my God, is with you. He will not fail you or forsake you until all the work for the service of the temple of the Lord is finished."

—— *DECLARATION OF FAITH* ——

My Father gives me understanding in all that He has called me to do. I am well able to accomplish every task that is set before me. I have no reason to fear or be dismayed. I am strong and very courageous. I will not forget that my Father God is with me in everything that I

*do. He will not fail me. He sees to it that I have all that I
need and stays with me as an ever-present help until all
of the work is finished.*

(1 Corinthians 2:6-16; 1 John 5:20; Daniel 1:17,20;
Joshua 1:5-9; Hebrews 13:5,6)

NEHEMIAH 9:17-21 KJV

And [they] refused to obey, neither were mindful of thy
wonders that thou didst among them; but hardened
their necks, and in their rebellion appointed a captain to
return to their bondage: but thou *art* a God ready to
pardon, gracious and merciful, slow to anger, and of
great kindness, and forsookest them not. Yea, when they
had made them a molten calf, and said, This is thy God
that brought thee up out of Egypt, and had wrought
great provocations; Yet thou in thy manifold mercies
forsookest them not in the wilderness: the pillar of the
cloud departed not from them by day, to lead them in
the way; neither the pillar of fire by night, to shew them
light, and the way wherein they should go. Thou gavest
also thy good spirit to instruct them, and withheldest
not thy manna from their mouth, and gavest them water
for their thirst. Yea, forty years didst thou sustain them
in the wilderness, *so that* they lacked nothing; their
clothes waxed not old, and their feet swelled not.

─────── *DECLARATION OF FAITH* ───────

My heavenly Father is forgiving and compassionate towards me. He grants me His unmerited favor as a free gift. His patience and love towards me have no end. He has given me His Word that He will never leave me nor forsake me.

Even when my faith has failed, He has remained faithful to me. He has never withheld His manna from my mouth and has always given me water for my thirst.

He has given me the Holy Spirit to instruct me in all of my ways.

He sustains me in every situation so that I lack no good thing. My clothes are not worn and ragged and my feet never swell from my journey in the life that He has called me to live.

(Psalm 103:1-18; Hebrews 13:5,6; John 16:13; Psalm 34:10; 106:45; Joel 2:13)

PSALM 77:3-14 KJV

I remembered God, and was troubled: I complained, and my spirit was overwhelmed. Selah. Thou holdest mine eyes waking: I am so troubled that I cannot speak. I have considered the days of old, the years of ancient times. I call to remembrance my song in the night: I commune with mine own heart: and my spirit made diligent search. Will the Lord cast off for ever? and will he be favourable no more? Is his mercy clean gone for ever? doth *his* promise fail for evermore? Hath God forgotten to be gracious? hath he in anger shut up his tender mercies? Selah. And I said, This *is* my infirmity: *but I will remember* the years of the right hand of the most High. I will remember the works of the Lord: surely I will remember thy wonders of old. I will meditate also of all thy work, and talk of thy doings. Thy way, O God, *is* in the sanctuary: who *is so* great a God as *our* God? Thou *art* the God that doest wonders: thou hast declared thy strength among the people.

—— *DECLARATION OF FAITH* ——

When hope seems lost and I begin to feel that God is indifferent to my needs, I will remember all that He has done in my life. When I am so troubled that I cannot even find the words to speak, I will remember His intervention in days of old. I will meditate upon His great works. I will remember the great salvation that He wrought for me. My Father is the Lord Most High. There is none greater than He. He will not forget me or leave me comfortless. He will act on my behalf.

(Psalm 22:1-5; Deuteronomy 7:17,18; Joshua 1:8; 2 Timothy 2:8-10)

LAMENTATIONS 3:22-26 KJV

It is of the Lord's mercies that we are not consumed, because his compassions fail not. *They are* new every morning: great *is* thy faithfulness. The Lord *is* my portion, saith my soul; therefore will I hope in him. The Lord *is* good unto them that wait for him, to the soul *that* seeketh him. *It is* good that *a man* should both hope and quietly wait for the salvation of the Lord.

———— *DECLARATION OF FAITH* ————

God's compassion for me never fails. He renews His love and blessings for me every morning and is faithful to fulfill the plan He has for my life.

I am His highest priority and He makes it His business to bless me.

He carefully watches over me so that I am not overrun by the enemy.

The Lord is my portion and my delight. I will wait for Him in the midst of adversity. I wait quietly for His salvation. He is always faithful and comes through for me every time.

God is not only good to me some of the time, He is good to me all of the time. He has given me His Word that He will never harm me in any way.

(Romans 8:38,39; Jeremiah 29:11; Isaiah 30:15; 40:28-31; Deuteronomy 6:24; Psalm 16:5; 78:38; 119:57,65)

PROTECTION

When I wrote the introduction in the love chapter on God giving us the ability to love others, this chapter on protection was in the back of my mind the whole time. Even though we are to love our enemies, sometimes we need to protect ourselves from them. That means that there are times when we should pray that they are even taken out of our way. That goes for enemies in this natural world as well as our spiritual enemies.

One name that comes to mind as a natural world enemy is Osama bin Laden. I hold fast to some of the following promises against him. I believe that he will be found out and utterly brought to justice. The Word teaches us that there are times when extreme measures are to be taken for the greater good. If an enemy threatens the life of your family, you protect your family first. They are what is most important.

This concept comes straight from the heart of your Father. If someone threatens His children, He takes it personally. He will protect you with a vengeance. The following promises are testimony to that fact.

EXODUS 12:12,13 AMP

I will pass through the land of Egypt this night and will smite all the firstborn in the land of Egypt, both man and beast; and against all the gods of Egypt I will execute judgment [proving their helplessness]. I am the Lord. The blood shall be for a token or sign to you upon [the doorposts of] the houses where you are, [that] when I see the blood, I will pass over you, and no plague shall be upon you to destroy you when I smite the land of Egypt.

———— DECLARATION OF FAITH ————

When the world is judged, I am not harmed. No plague can come upon me to destroy me, for I am covered with the blood of the Lamb!

(John 5:24; Psalm 91; 1 Peter 1:18,19; Exodus 15:26; 1 Corinthians 5:7)

2 SAMUEL 8:6 NKJV

Then David put garrisons in Syria of Damascus; and the Syrians became David's servants, *and* brought tribute. The Lord preserved David wherever he went.

———— DECLARATION OF FAITH ————

The Lord preserves and protects me. He keeps me safe from harm and destruction.

He is with me always and gives me victory wherever I go.

(Psalm 23; 91; Romans 8:37; 2 Corinthians 2:14; Deuteronomy 32:38)

JOB 1:10-11 NKJV

"Have You not made a hedge around him, around his household, and around all that he has on every side? You have blessed the work of his hands, and his possessions have increased in the land. But now, stretch out Your hand and touch all that he has, and he will surely curse You to Your face!"

—— *DECLARATION OF FAITH* ——

God has placed a hedge of protection around my family, myself, and everything that I have, and the enemy cannot penetrate it no matter how hard he tries.

The Lord blesses all of the work of my hands, making me prosperous and very wealthy.

(Psalm 5:11,12; 34:7; 112:1-3; Job 3:23; 1 John 5:18; Deuteronomy 8:18; 28:12)

LUKE 21:17-19 KJV

Ye shall be hated of all *men* for my name's sake. But there shall not an hair of your head perish. In your patience possess ye your souls.

—— *DECLARATION OF FAITH* ——

I am not concerned by the hatred that comes my way because of my love and devotion to Jesus. I know that not a hair on my head will perish, for I have God's unfailing Word that He will protect me at all times.

By my steadfast and patient endurance I win vitality for my soul.

(Romans 1:16; Psalm 91; Exodus 23:20-23; Matthew 10:22,30)

2 THESSALONIANS 3:3 NIV

The Lord is faithful, and he will strengthen and protect you from the evil one.

—— *DECLARATION OF FAITH* ——

The Lord is faithful. He strengthens me with His awesome power and protects me from the strategies of the evil one. My heavenly Father takes His stand as a sentinel in my life. He is ever-alert and well able to maintain His covenant with me and bring me to victory in every situation.

(1 Thessalonians 5:24; Luke 10:17-19; Psalm 91;
1 Corinthians 1:9; John 17:15)

REST AND REJUVENATION

So many people, especially in the ministry, become obsessed with their work. They lose sight of the joys of living and the result is often failed health, failed marriages, friendships dissolved, etc. God did not intend for you to be so unbalanced in your career. He did not create you to be a workaholic. He wants you to have regular rest so that life isn't so overwhelming. God himself rested on the seventh day. Jesus even commanded His disciples to take a break and relax in spite of all the work that had to be done.

There are also promises here of restful sleep. God wants you to feel so secure about your life that nothing brings you anxiety. When you sleep it should be sweet, so that when you awake, you are refreshed and ready to meet a new day.

1 KINGS 8:56 KJV

Blessed *be* the Lord, that hath given rest unto his people Israel, according to all that he promised: there hath not failed one word of all his good promise, which he promised by the hand of Moses his servant.

─────── *DECLARATION OF FAITH* ───────

The Lord has given me rest.
All of His promises to me are manifested in my life.
None of His promises fail me. Not one word that my
Father has spoken to me fails to come to pass.

(Deuteronomy 12:10; Hebrews 3; 2 Corinthians 1:20;
Isaiah 55:11)

PSALM 4:8 NKJV

I will both lie down in peace, and sleep;
For You alone, O Lord, make me dwell in safety.

─────── *DECLARATION OF FAITH* ───────

I will lie down and sleep in perfect peace—safe and
secure in the arms of my heavenly Father.

(Psalm 3:5; Leviticus 25:18; Deuteronomy 12:10; 33:12;
Ephesians 2:14)

JEREMIAH 6:16 AMP

Thus says the Lord: Stand by the roads and look; and ask
for the eternal paths, where the good, old way is; then

walk in it, and you will find rest for your souls. But they said, We will not walk in it!

——— *DECLARATION OF FAITH* ———

I walk in ways tested and tried—ways that bring honor and glory to my Father and ultimately lead me to true rest.

(Psalm 119:89-93,140; Ephesians 5:1-18; Matthew 11:29)

MATTHEW 11:27-30 KJV

All things are delivered unto me of my Father: and no man knoweth the Son, but the Father; neither knoweth any man the Father, save the Son, and *he* to whomsoever the Son will reveal *him*. Come unto me, all *ye* that labour and are heavy laden, and I will give you rest. Take my yoke upon you, and learn of me; for I am meek and lowly in heart: and ye shall find rest unto your souls. For my yoke *is* easy, and my burden is light.

——— *DECLARATION OF FAITH* ———

I am born to fully know and accurately understand the things of God. Jesus, my Lord and my brother, has given me a thorough revelation of our Father's being.

I cast all of the heavy burdens of my life upon Jesus. They are now upon His shoulders and I am set free. All that has weighed me down is now His to bear.

I have taken His yoke upon me and have made Him the center of all of my learning. I find comfort in His gentleness and simplicity. In Him, I have found rest, relief, and refreshment for my soul.

The yoke that I have been given is easy to bear. It is life to me in abundance.

(1 Corinthians 2:6-16; 1 John 5:20; 1 Peter 5:5-7; John 6:35-37; 10:10)

MARK 6:31 NKJV

[Jesus] said to them, "Come aside by yourselves to a deserted place and rest a while." For there were many coming and going, and they did not even have time to eat.

—— *DECLARATION OF FAITH* ——

I will not allow life to become so hectic for me that I have no leisure time. It is not the will of my Father that I be overwhelmed that way. Therefore, I will regularly take time to rest and enjoy the blessings that He has given me.

(Ecclesiastes 2:24; 3:22; Matthew 11:28-30; 14:13)

PRAYER OF SALVATION

God loves you—no matter who you are, no matter what your past. God loves you so much that He gave His one and only begotten Son for you. The Bible tells us that "…whoever believes in him shall not perish but have eternal life" (John 3:16 NIV). Jesus laid down His life and rose again so that we could spend eternity with Him in heaven and experience His absolute best on earth. If you would like to receive Jesus into your life, say the following prayer out loud and mean it from your heart:

> *Heavenly Father, I come to You admitting that I am a sinner. Right now, I choose to turn away from sin, and I ask You to cleanse me of all unrighteousness. I believe that Your Son, Jesus, died on the cross to take away my sins. I also believe that He rose again from the dead so that I might be forgiven of my sins and made righteous through faith in Him. I call upon the name of Jesus Christ to be the Savior and Lord of my life. Jesus, I choose to follow You and ask that You fill me with the power of the Holy Spirit. I declare that right now I am a child of God. I am free from sin and full of the right-eousness of God. I am saved in Jesus' name. Amen.*

If you prayed this prayer to receive Jesus Christ as your Savior for the first time, please contact us on the web at **www.harrisonhouse.com** to receive a free book.

Or you may write to us at

Harrison House
P.O. Box 35035
Tulsa, Oklahoma 74153

ABOUT THE AUTHOR

James Riddle is a successful entrepreneur, educator, and Bible teacher. His unique approach to writing stirs the heart and encourages the soul. One does not have to sit under his teaching for long to know that he has a deep love for the body of Christ. It is pure joy for him to see God's children living in closeness with their Father and fulfilling the call He has on their lives.

At the center of all of James' success is his love for the Word. "In my own personal life," he says, "I have a simple mission statement. 'Be the person you are created to be.'" It is his resolute conviction that only through the Word can anyone achieve true success and be the person that God wants them to be. Therefore, the Word must always be our final authority, no matter what we are facing.

It is just that attitude that caused James to write *The Complete Personalized Promise Bible.* For three and a half years he researched and personalized everything the Bible says about who we are, what we have, and how we are supposed to act as Christians. It was birthed in a determination to believe the right things so he could keep his prayers in the perfect will of God. All of that research and dedication is now available to the public, and what a blessing it is!

James holds an honors degree in Creative Writing from the University of Texas at El Paso. His *Complete Personalized Promise Bible* series has sold well over 100,000 copies. He is the father of four and lovingly refers to his wife, Jinny, as his beautiful Puerto Rican princess.

James Riddle would love to hear how God has blessed you through this material. Please send your testimony to the following address:

James Riddle Ministries
P.O. Box 972624
El Paso, Texas 79997

Or email him at:
thepromisecenter@elp.rr.com

Visit James Riddle online at:
www.jamesriddle.net

EVERY PROMISE IN THE BIBLE IN TOPICAL FORMAT JUST FOR MEN!

This easy-to-use topical edition for men gives them all the promises specially designed for their needs. Each Scripture is personalized just like the original version and includes inspiring devotional introductions to each topic. Selected topics include:

Your Call to Leadership

Guidance

Faith

Prosperity

Knowing Your Destiny in Life

Wisdom

And more!

A powerful and life-changing gift, this unique book is perfect for yourself and others!

The Complete Personalized Promise Bible for Men
By James Riddle
ISBN 13: 978-1-57794-663-2

Available at fine bookstores everywhere
or visit www.harrisonhouse.com.

ALL THE PROMISES FOR WOMEN IN AN EASY-TO-USE TOPICAL FORMAT!

Now women can find every promise in the Bible by topic in this specially designed edition. Each Scripture is personalized just like the original version and includes inspiring devotional introductions to each topic. Selected topics include:

Freedom From Fear

Encouragement

Long Life

A Successful Marriage

Children

Peace

Protection

And more!

This unique and inspiring book is perfect as a treasured gift for yourself or someone you love.

The Complete Personalized Promise Bible for Women

By James Riddle

ISBN 13: 978-1-57794-664-2

Available at fine bookstores everywhere
or visit www.harrisonhouse.com.

DISCOVER GOD'S PURPOSE AND PROMISES FOR YOUR FINANCIAL LIFE!

For the first time, you can find every promise from God's Word about your financial life in one handy resource. You'll find every Bible promise on finances along with a powerful declaration of faith and a conversational prayer for you to speak directly from your heart to the heart of God. Selected topics include:

Debt	Generosity
Success	Investing
Saving	Crises
Budgeting	Greed
Ministry	

This simple yet potent tool will help you unleash the power of faith and prayer in your life right now and help

you receive the financial blessings God has for you today.

The Complete Personalized Promise Bible on Financial Increase

By James Riddle

ISBN 13: 978-1-57794-779-0

Available at fine bookstores everywhere
or visit www.harrisonhouse.com.

HEALING BELONGS TO YOU!

With over 100,000 of *The Complete Personalized Promise Bibles* sold, now every single promise for health and healing in the Bible is compiled in one convenient volume. Not only are these Scripture promises listed for you, but each one is accompanied by a personalized prayer and declaration of faith.

You'll discover that Jesus died to bring wholeness in every area of your life. Broken relationship and fellowship with God has now been restored. Sickness is now healed. As you review these powerful Scriptures, pray in faith, and declare the Word, the light of God's love will begin to bring healing to your life.

Recognize His love for you in its fullest measure

and discover that no sin, sickness, or disease will ever hold you in bondage again.

The Complete Personalized Promise Bible on Health and Healing

By James Riddle

ISBN 13: 978-1-57794-840-7

Available at fine bookstores everywhere
or visit www.harrisonhouse.com.

Fast. Easy.
Convenient.

For the latest Harrison House product information and author news, look no further
than your computer. All the details on our
powerful, life-changing products are just a
click away. New releases, E-mail
subscriptions, Podcasts, testimonies,
monthly specials—find it all in one place.
Visit harrisonhouse.com today!

harrisonhouse

THE HARRISON HOUSE VISION

Proclaiming the truth and the power
Of the Gospel of Jesus Christ
With excellence;

Challenging Christians to
Live victoriously,
Grow spiritually,
Know God intimately.